Who Will Care About An American

K.M. KENNEDY

WHO WILL CARE ABOUT AN AMERICAN

A BOOK FOR THOSE OF YOUTH

2007

Who Will Care About An American

GOOD TIMES

"…or struggle just like Flo and James Evans." *These words from Alicia play in my head and* I think how glad I am that after all these years, finally the show Good Times comes on in my area in re-runs. It's been years. Years since I saw this show that relates so closely to my child hood. Every one I knew it seems, lived this way. It all starts in the projects and those roots never leave you if you have them. Something in your progressing life may tell you to leave it, but those roots don't go away. You still remember rubbing together paper bags for toilet paper, and boiling water when the hot water goes, or opening the stove for heat, or eating grits and oatmeal or cream of wheat on the regular, and those holiday dinners where the menu hardly varied from one holiday to the next, collard greens, macaroni and cheese, ham, potato salad, sweet potato pie, and some other stuff, but these were the main staples. There were house parties, drunken grown ups, kids stealing beer and liquor from the bar or kitchen. And the MUSIC. Blues, R & B, Motown, Disco, Aretha Franklin, Gladys Knight & the Pips, Al Green, Marvin Gaye, Muddy Waters, Donna Summer, Gloria Gaynor, and a slew of one hit wonders of the time. And you were a child. And even though your father was mean like James and your mother mild like Flo, at least this was my case, you have your friends, who are your cousins too and you make fun of it all, together. And when you become old enough, after going to public school all your life, you miss it.

It and school were two very different things. Slowly the fun and dreams you weave from your home environment are being consistently, formulaically, methodically, secretly and shamefully taken away from you, in the assimilation, normalization process, that is public school. And over that rich canvas of color and spirit and family, and fun and ideas and dreams, after a period of years, the paint brush does its white wash job. Turns you against your own and teaches you prescribed better things. Always hinting that what you are learning is better.

I say, after learning how to read, write, and count, and if you don't have a fascination with science, school has done its job. Because that history they taught us, back in my day, left out a lot, has since changed factually, and was down right full of slanted lies. Beyond geography, it's not that useful. If I used the history facts I learned in school all those years ago to debate with today, I'd surely lose. And you'd swear from that one paragraph about blacks in the 1960's Revolution period, that Martin Luther King was the only voice that existed. And that one big fact about Columbus discovering America, and Indians and Pilgrims and the Thanksgiving feast become hard to swallow over time.

However, we moved from the projects to the house up the hill. But the projects are still where I went to play. It's where my relatives and friends were. But, we were now different because we got out. We were rich or something. People began to act differently. The Grown ups. But even though, I still hung out in the projects for years.

My life starts to over lap with other experiences. And I would learn that life would just continually overlap, until some things faded away to memory as other things took a firmer hold.

We began to make friends, thanks to school, with children in our new area. Other children who lived in houses too. Some originally from the projects, some not. And as children we were all the same. We still all liked to play, and dream, and make up stuff and fight. We were creative. We had shows. We built boxing rings. We formed singing groups and dance groups and drill teams in our off hours from school. And slowly we grew up and lost it all. All the vim and vigor. All of the fun was replaced with the agenda of the school. Become serious about life. These are the steps. You have to do it and you have to do it this way if you want to succeed in life. You're going to need to be prepared to be a worker bee in a factory or a corporation. They require this or that. Forget you. That's what school is meant for. It's meant for you to forget you and become them.

And slowly the agenda of the school overtook me. My parents being from a prior time and place, when education was hard to come by and hard to finish, and sometimes cost a fee, believed in the school's overall purpose. Since life had been so hard for them, they bought in that education was the way to go, and so as a child with two strong entities supporting the wonder and ability of a school and it's overall purpose of making children into proper useful citizens for society, surely I went along for their pleasure, and I wound up liking it. There was an element of competitiveness that made it fun. Getting the best grade, or drawing the better picture or reading a paragraph perfectly, or spelling all 20 words correctly on a spelling test, or completing 50 multiplication problems the quickest. Yeah I began to love it like a game. Like a competitor. Later, valedictorian, awards, trophies, scholarships, all wonderful things in that game. And then it's over.

But back to my beginning. The 60's revolution in America, changed the way whites and blacks were allowed to legally interact with one another. People had to be respectful of one another regardless of sex or race. And growing up a child in the seventies, you could feel the mood intensely. As a black child you knew white was considered better and black inferior. And I'm sure vice versa. There was an incident when I was in the 1st or second grade, when two white women knocked at my classroom door and asked the teacher to speak with me. My teacher asked that I go outside the classroom and speak with them. The funny thing after the incident is that they didn't even talk with my parents first or never afterward. They just did this thing that I'll never forget.

Anyway, by urban school standards, I was a smart child showing early promise and was somehow chosen by some committee of which these two white ladies represented. They flattered my accomplishments and then laid it on me. "How would you like to be the only black girl at so and so school?" Because I don't remember now the school. But they said it just like that. Not at all appealing. Kind of scary, and since they gave me a choice, of course I said no. And that was the end of it. I went home and told my mother and she seemed not to care so much. It passed. But there would be many other condescending situations like this to follow for many years after this incident.

At this stage in life, I was learning it would seem, that the only goal a black person should or would have, is to be as good as, or like a white person. That would become all of our missions. This is how these incidents made me feel. And either consciously or subconsciously, not being quite sure sometimes, because it could have been peer pressure, or sheer competitiveness, or something else, but anyway you look at it, it was all engendered by white is right mentality, that I think I did make my mission to be like them. To have what they had, live how they live, work at the jobs they work at, at least by TV standards. But all the while I felt different. Even though I made that a goal, I truly felt different. I didn't really feel like that, but I made it a goal. And even though there were successful black people on TV and other media, I chose white. Like choosing a white doll over a black doll. We learn young.

My life just keeps on overlapping. Some things stay, some become memories. Just like the projects were a root in me, so has the white black issue become one.

WARNING

But all of this pales in comparison to where I and most other Americans, both black and white, find themselves today. America is rooted in me. What it was, is, can, and will become. And it can become one of two things. Wrong or right. American history is rooted in me. This is my home. I live here on this soil. Thinking and breathing. This is my home and it is my duty to be protective of it. It is my duty to recognize its being led astray. It is my duty to voice my dismay and as the pundits like to say, open a dialogue. These people we've let become in charge; who we give control of our governance, and the keys to the candy store, have got to become accountable for their wickedness. Republican, Democrat, it doesn't matter. They're all the same, cut from the same cloth, but if you give them the opportunity, they will take those two words and try to divide the country up with them. Into just those two categories, as if you could truly do something like that with a human mind. Like corporations they've become brand crazy. I'm not a brand. I'm not Democrat or Republican. I don't advertise for either. If truth be told, I dislike both brands. Can't we come up with another?

We've got this election process, that dwindles the candidate pool to just one representative of each brand and then they put that candidate into the republican or democratic machinery, called a party, and all their millions in resources go to that one candidate. I often wonder why this is so. Why can't there be seventeen candidates or 100, all the way down to the finish line, who choose not to be a part of either party and their millions in resources, but who recognize that there are actually people they should represent and not a party?

***

I don't want to quote research materials, but I have done mine. To my satisfaction. And I have become distressed. In addition to taking a time out from the rigors of being a cog in the system, and re introducing common sense and reasoning to my thinking mechanism, (something I seemed to have lost the ability to do since either primary or secondary school), the manner of my research happens to be newspapers, periodicals, TV, TV news, both network and cable, local, national and international in some cases, and more than anything, I came away from it all not feeling knowledgeable of anything worth knowing, but more sensitive to reality and truth.

Don't expect this work to enlighten you with lots of hard statistical fact. In fact, I hate statistics. Statistics leave no room for individuals or miracles. Statistics close you up in a jail of cause and effect. Expectancy of an outcome because of an input. It allows no room for change. And if a miracle did get through, it would be labeled an aberration, plus or minus 2 percentage points for error. It's a mind thing. If you eat statistics, you'll certainly become a stupid computer. So young people, take heed while you have a chance. Use your own mind and don't give it away to the statisticians. It will be your duty to save America in the near future. Don't be led astray.

In the sixties, the youth recognized something like this. They became dis- illusioned with the two parties, the rhetoric the parties were feeding and the reality that their rhetoric was creating. They noticed a disparity between the two. But to quell the uprising, the two parties joined together and pulled out their most powerful weapon. The following short story will sum up the results of their battle:

<u>GOT THE MESSAGE, MISSED THE CALL</u>

Customer Service Worker I: I've got this 63 year old woman on the line screaming at me. Can you hear her?"

Customer Service Worker II: Yeah, I hear her.

(Thanks to technology, and the Age of Information, Customer Service Worker I was reading the lady's curriculum vitae, while the lady impatiently held the phone. The old lady thought she was checking her account history.)

Customer Service Worker I: Okay, let me get back to her.
"Miss I'm sorry I can't help you."

Retired Lady: What do you mean you can't help me. I'm entitled to this program. I've put my time in as a working, contributing, citizen of this society, and up until last month I've never had a problem receiving my retirement benefits."

Customer Service Worker I: I've reviewed your account and it appears that your generation, the baby boomers, started a lovely revolution that could have saved our present fate in this world, but you allowed yourselves to be bought off by the elite instead. Thus we all became slaves because at that watershed moment, you all turned into marshmallows. You even agreed to turn your kids into marshmallows.

You craved safety, comfort, and security, for each of you individually, and in return you bargained our freedom by writing and supporting many laws that stifled succeeding generations. How'd you turn on your own ideas?

Retired Lady: What are you talking about? What's this got to do with my money?

Customer Service Worker I: Ah, how quickly and easily we forget. But you do remember it's time for you to collect! You're free. It's your children and your childrens' children, that have become slaves. You've been manipulated by money to help the elite carry out their master plan of world domination through market globalization. You could have toppled the corporation, who to appease you, *and legally, they are a who,* made you think they cared all those years ago, then they pounced on your minds for a whole generation, only to take it from you; To throw you and your kids away in favor of foreigners, who were more. More eager, and more smarter because the elite worked hard through the marshmallow laws you helped to create, to dumb down our schools by placating the whims of your children because they wanted your children placated. They kept you out of your homes and away from your kids who needed you to raise them. And fooled you with the illusion two can make more money, only to go up on the price of everything, and put a price on everything. And you revolutionaries bought it. And sold us. You sold our future. And you are the age of those in power now and you're still selling our future, because that's what you do. You baby boomers sell futures. Stock market futures and human futures. And now you have more human futures than ever before to sell. You've got the whole world. And we're so stupid we'll follow in your footsteps. Letting the state, in the form of public education raise our kids to become slaves, while the two of us as parents are already enslaved nine or more hours a day. Tired, frantic, unable to live, unable to use our minds because we don't have time. We only have time to work, sleep and eat. To keep up with bill payments and stupidly keep making bills to feed the appetite of the credit king. The smooth talking, enticing fella that he is.

Your revolution, helped to do away with the remaining vestiges of organized African American slavery in this country, but in exchange you sold your kids, because somebody's gotta do the work. You didn't know it but you sold your kids into slavery when you stopped being vigilant. You got comfortable and you stopped being vigilant. Fell right into your places in the wrong line. Shame on you!

To sum it up, the 'they' you fought against, bought and placated you, in exchange for your children, and their children and so on.

And all you care about now is medicaid and medicare and your social security checks from the government. You soldiers on the wrong side! You all should get everything you want. But they're throwing you away now. You make up a big chunk of the population and quite frankly you've become a drain on resources. You won't die, thanks to advancement in technology and medicine. One would think they'd stop advancing in these areas, just to get rid of you through attrition. But the flip side is they get to take the money they give you back from you most often in the form of medicine and hospital visits. Sometimes technology. Y'all don't seem all that keen on the technology.

I'm angry with you. Because you sold us, when you could have changed the direction of the world. And so no, I can't help you."

Retired Lady: I'm sorry. My generation did do that."

(Shocked by the old lady's response, the customer service rep's words lost momentum.
The old lady wasn't supposed to agree.)

Customer Service Worker I: Ma'm, one moment
And she took the block off of her account.

Because some of us now, who are angry, with our threatened minimum wage jobs, do that to the old people in jest, just to induce such a phone call. The calls don't always run this smoothly though. We usually get stopped in mid sentence. The old people call us crazy and foolish. They tell us we've got our facts wrong. We don't know what we're talking about, etc. etc. But at that moment, during a phone call like this, we have power, so when they disagree it doesn't matter. It's just going to take them that much longer to get their monies. But this old lady cried UNCLE.

***

For their compliance, this prior generation got retirement plans, pension plans, medical coverage, insurance, job stability for all their working years, and this overall sense of entitlement. Their children, nothing. They didn't take care of us, yet we'll be administering to their needs until they die. And as they fed themselves and left us nothing, so we have nothing to feed our children in the way of the formula of stable living. All we can do is turn them out into a world overrun by greed, and controlled now by our parents' generation, who have become like those before them.

A Word on Medical Care and Coverage

Since healthcare has been mentioned, let's stay here a moment. Used to be, you paid into a plan provided by your employer. You got an insurance card and used it at the doctor's office. A copay was unheard of. In the case of my family we paid 20 percent and the health care provider paid 80 percent. Period. Then enter, late eighties, early nineties; a new industry. Consortiums of managed health care professionals whose mission would become to manage health care. Doctors were corralled into care networks. Organization of services based on statistics and science, by these health care managers, were created. Reduced choices. Doctor's abilities were reduced to what the managed care plan decided they should be for specific symptoms and circumstances. And they introduced expensive copays (possibly to deter visits because managed health care is a bottom line business).

Now one pays into the employer plan, which at the very basic of coverage allows for 2 teeth cleanings and a physical for free. After this, an enormous thousands of dollars deductible program, which effectively makes health care insurance useless, but pre tax PSA savings accounts were offered by the federal government as a sort of tax break to blunt the affects of having to effectively have to pay out of pocket for your own health care. Other plans are offered that cover more with less of a deductible if you don't mind spending your whole paycheck to finance it, but hey!!!!

MORE IMPORTANT THERE STILL IS NO CURE FOR CANCER. Not even close. What are the professionals in the medical profession working on all these years. Healthcare costs are at an all time high, but barring pill cocktails for comfort and new gadgets to take the place of real body parts, there's still no healing. They've come up with nothing worthwhile or new in the form of cures and fixes for the body.

WHAT HAPPENED TO THE IMAGE OF AMERICA?

_"Goodnight song. Played so wrong. Blame the crowd, who screamed so loud so long."

Tears for Fears

As I sit hit here, hopefully like most normal Americans. I can't help but feel so unattached to this Iraq debacle. It's like a game unfolding terribly wrong for the Americans. A game being played by the powers, that have set themselves above the people they were supposed to serve. Infighting with each other and outfighting with Internationals. Just plain looking bad. Giving all the heads and ruler of other countries fodder to throw back at us. To wag their fingers and chide the "Americans". Except I am one American that didn't ask for all of this. They are not representing me and hopefully they aren't representing any other normal person in this country. I am just appalled. I am embarrassed and I know that every normal American will have to pay in the future for what has happened. For the underlying motives that are being revealed. Once this country had our emotion, It had our inattentiveness and full support that they would do what was right . They would do what was best for this country and its citizens. They kept us busy with color coded alerts. New products and other gadgetry, as well as sensationalized headlines of entertainers and sports figures whose lives had gone awry. Non stop they tried to focus our attention everywhere except on what they were actually doing. They still think we care about such things, as evidenced by the ridiculous coverage of the tawdry life and death of Anna Nicole Smith. Giving her no peace even in death. Or the non stop harassment of Brittany Spears. But what has really been happening is this:

Do our leaders really look concerned? They don't even look concerned. They all look like business and lately they've been looking like business running out of time. While we were all supposed to still be overwhelmingly affected by the 9/11 of the year 2001, and it is now 2007, so they think, our politicians have been quite busy, removing our freedoms, selling away our country in backroom deals, burdening regular Americans with the greedy wants of Corporations, and sticking the American people with huge tabs to pay for the dishonesty in the handling of natural disaster debacles like hurricane Katrina and Rita, and war and war rebuilding contracts given to their friends, and just the overall funding of every policing effort across the whole world. These leaders will all be gone tomorrow, with the fattest pockets ever; by the way they've even been forced to rat and turn on business allies and other political allies, once their wrong doings were brought to light. If these were their friends then surely they can be judged by the company they kept. They're all criminals in one form or another. They've all been drunken by the power they keep trying to increase, while they feed us war emotions and evoke 9/11 like remember the Alamo, and we are supposed to click into line. They swear they are protecting us and our borders but our ports were almost run by Dubai, we have a border problem and are supposedly overrun by illegal immigrants. We have no jobs. Employers don't want to pay. All the money (disposable income) in this country is tied up in the hands of a few. The budget deficit is at an all time high, and we lazy Americans keep trodding along as if there is nothing the masses can do to stop this. To stop the powers who are supposed to be serving us. It is time for a new song in America.

I know we've all heard it before, but let's hear it again. Who do wars serve? Please think about this and find out the answer if you don't know it already. In a time like the times we are in, when humans seemed to have mastered their highest level of civility toward one another, why would a war have to occur? The people who attacked our nation on 9/11, represented no one country. But we could all understand invading Afghanistan because it was *proven* that this is where they were hiding out. It was confirmed by worldwide intelligence. But why on earth did we invade Iraq. Why did we cause the death of multiple times more of its citizens than Sadaam Hussein ever did in his whole regime? Why are we still there? Are we trying for the ultimate prize? And what is that ultimate prize? Democracy in the region? Like we really care about that!

It is disheartening to read in the paper how Russian (ex Soviet Union) generals feel about us fighting against this sort of 'enemy'. They say their heart goes out to our soldiers who are fighting a losing battle and dying in vain. And how do they know? They were once in this same position (but they were trying to hold together an empire). And at that time the US was against the Soviet Union, and helping the very same kind of people we find ourselves fighting against today. Even though there is a little jabbing in this sentiment, I still find some sincerity from the Russian generals, especially toward the way America is using its military.

But the point is, when will we all learn? When will we change this song?

***

It sucks to be on the losing team. When I was growing up, people all over the world seemed to like Americans. We were trying to be a better people. What happened?

Overnight, we became the scourge of the global community it seems. People all over the world hate us. What is responsible for this?

The short answer is, **those other people**. Those faceless, legal, human entities, with branded names, called corporations. You've got human people and you've got corporation people. Funny thing, these make believe, oligarchies actually, have all the say and the real humans have none. They have the ability to outlive any human being. We work for them, we rely on them for wages and a livelihood, news, education, entertainment, everything!!!!! How ridiculous is that? Are we capable of doing anything on our own? When did we lose ourselves so completely to corporations? Is it because we can't see their faces that we don't think of them as people? Law says they're people. We'd better start treating them as such. Because these people have been running the world quite visibly for the past few decades, enslaving all the fleshy bodies all over the globe and bending them to their will. We'd better think twice before we let them grow so big. And they've got a lot of that powerful weapon that the parties have, and just like the parties placated the 'revolutionaries', the corporations placate the parties. If American corporations make bold decisions that affect the entire world, either for good or bad, it's the American flesh and the American country that they hide behind. They're the spawn run amuck. They make alliances with others of their kind, in other countries. They band together by industry, to effect common outcomes for their product across the whole world, in their pursuit to acquire more, if not all, of the powerful weapon. They mutate into hybrids and conglomerations before any human is aware, picking up prestige and power along the way. They're parasitic, and when they've exhausted all their options in the host country, they move on to another, then the other, and....I think they're in India and China now.

Corporations

Are organizations, of people, who are organized, and who organize. They take on a whole new form and overall vision or view of things for profit. They become an entity all unto themselves. And they continue organizing, which is the problem. They never stop.

They organize people, materials, resources, everything on earth and they don't stop. They assign to everything a monetary value, and they never stop the process of organizing. The whole earth shall soon be organized to the nth degree. Homogenous, spiceless, uneventful., predictable.

I'm not saying it's good or bad, they teach us to be organized. But I realize all this organization can be damaging. Sterilizing. Personally at home I'm a pack rat.

If we have to be beholden to corporations to organize our life structure and for support then track their doings. Learn about them to see where you stand. Don't just listen to words. Stay on top of the news, read many different sources, some know better than others.

Who's fault is this? It is the politicians' fault, for favoring corporate humans over human humans. How do the politicians get into office? We elect them. Why do they betray us? Acquisition of the powerful weapon. How does this happen? Read the Abramoff Chronicles currently offered in news.

Someone wrote a book recently called *The World Is Flat*. Immediately politicians who we thought served us, because we elected them, embraced this philosophy as an explanation to be fed to the American human humans as to why we're feeling that sort of let down way we feel lately. Heeding us to reconcile ourselves to the new reality of the revelations of this book.

As proof of this new philosophical adoption, I offer a full article in the Charlotte Observer newspaper yesterday, from the AP, reformatted and retyped to fit this page:

Bangalore, India—Sen. Max Baucus, the top democrat on the U. S.

Finance Committee, said Friday that outsourcing white-collar jobs to low countries such as India has become a global fact of life—and that America must learn to live with it.

The Senator from Montana also called on India to further open its once- Tightly closed economy, especially in the agricultural and retail Industries, to competition from U.S. companies.

Baucus said a majority of fellow Senate Democrats agreed with him, Despite the party's longtime opposition to American companies Moving jobs overseas.

"Everybody is concerned about job losses and so am I," he told

the Associated Press in an interview in Bangalore, his first stop on a five-day tour of India.

"But **the world is flat** and we must work harder to better retrain our people," rather than resist outsourcing, he said. "Offs-shoring is a fact of globalization. **Opportunities for U. S. companies come from every where—including India.**"

Charlotte's big banks are among the American firms sending work to India. Bank of America has 1500 employees in a subsidiary in Mumbai (formerly Bombay) and Hyderabad. Wachovia has been outsourcing technology and other business processes to contractors in India.

In a written statement Friday, Baucus said the intent of his trip was to "try To get at the problem of outsourcing" and find ways to keep them At home by boosting America's competitiveness through such things as Training, education and tax incentives."

Contracts from foreign firms for everything from software engineering to customer service call centers has helped turn India's economy into one Of the world's fastest growing. Outsourcing is expected to bring in $22 billion in revenues this fiscal year.

Critics say outsourcing puts skilled people out of work just so big Companies can save money. Supporters argue that it actually creates Jobs by helping companies grow faster.

On Friday, Baucus cited the prosperity that outsourcing has brought to Bangalore, India's technology hub, and it served as a showcase for grow- ing ties between the two countries. And he said a reciprocal open- ing of markets would benefit both the United States and India.

And I say, okay, corporate American humans are satisfied, but what about me, the actual American human? Why does my lifestyle have to be ruined to further their satisfaction?

This is the reality, so we'd better get used to it! I have a question. Are these other countries primary patrons of these businesses or are they just serving to reduce costs to the corporations? 'They' set America up for a certain standard of living, of which prices have only been increasing, and they don't want Americans to have these jobs anymore, nor lower their prices. They even go so far as to torture Americans with the fear of job loss. De-stabilizing our whole lives.

Not to mention the education factor. Our populace has deliberately not been kept up to pace as to be able to function in these types of jobs so they don't have to go 'off-shore' to a smarter people? What the hell is going on! We have to be retrained? We were told over the years we were the greatest, richest, most powerful, nation on earth. Would someone please explain how we got here, if what this senator is saying is true! This just all seems so deliberate to me. How hard is it to answer the phone, pull up an account and relay information? I smiled a big smile of disbelief and gratification over the fact that these fools don't know the truth of the matter. The truth of the matter is Americans can say f——- this, and f——- you, and corporate goals and lies. Neither of you get to tell us who we are, and least of all to tell us we are incompetent, when we relied on your good judgment in the past where education and formulaic success were concerned. Now you all want to blame it on us? We should have never trusted you, but we didn't know not to, as aggressively as we shouldn't have. You corporations had always been around. You seemed to do good by our fathers....

The truth is also, we probably won't.

And the answer to the title is politicians sold us out in favor of corporations. With great enticements, of course, but they sold our image a way. What's an American these days? Where can you find one?

DISTRACTIONS FROM THE TRUTH

The Age of Information

The age of information
Will be the ruin
Of a nation

Everything said, done,
What one thinks,
Individual fun

Will all be spun
And spent
Then sent as information

Everything thought, believed,
Eaten, used, or breathed
Will be over interpreted,
Over analyzed and
Over sold

As things everyone should know

Mutated ideas will form
From misguided CRAP
Overemphasis will make
Sure of that

Some people are still talking about the American Dream. I'm wondering and feeling that it's dead. But that empty step by step formula still seems to be around. 'Get a good education', which will lead to a good career, work hard, get a house, have a family, and acquire some stuff. (all of it, barring the job, preferably on credit).

The people who still believe this are distracted by tabloid news stories, racy TV and electronic gadgets. What's an IPOD? A glorified walkman. Playstation? A time consumption piece. A camera phone? Just plain unnecessary. A TV? The grand disseminator of popular culture which tells us to buy these stupid things, as well as how to live, who and what to love, who and what to hate, and how to think, and how to think about what they tell us to think about.

It's not about hard work anymore. If you want 'it', you can buy it, and some financial institution will finance it for you, no matter who you are or how imprudent it would be to do so. Just keep buying 'it' and you'll be serving your country. America, as it stands today, your job is to spend spend spend. Spend what you do have, spend what you don't have, it's okay, you'll just pledge your futures on your excess. Your future is good for it. After 9/11, the president even urged us to keep on spending. So if you plan to be a spend -a -holic, consider your future American. Like whether or not you'll have a job in this country.

And while you're distracted, trying to decide what new, lovely, innovation to purchase, unknown bills and laws get passed, that come to light only when you've been caught in their snare. Like, lopsided trade laws with foreign countries, and Patriot Acts that reduce your freedom.

There's a commercial with a guy on a riding lawn mower, pointing out the wonderful things he's purchased, and he ends it with "I'm in debt up to my eyeballs. I can hardly keep up with my finance charges. Somebody help me." And I believe there's a lending company that offers him a hand, in the form of more debt, probably spread out over a longer period of time.

In the ancient days, a person saw a plot of land, cut down some trees and built him an abode. The abode, maybe with some add-ons from time to time, sufficed for life. Roots were formed, care and concern for the land and so forth,

Enter today:

Builder + Skill, labor, material = house for sale

How does one buy the house? **With something of equal value to trade,**
Or a universal medium of exchange backed by something of real value.

Enter Money (however no longer backed by real value, instead sanctioned to be created through strict rules and regulations, but as long as they are adhered to, you can create as much of it as you want if you're a banker)

Enter Banks (following the strict guidelines for money creation, while at the same time receiving back some of that creation from depositors, who have received it for wages earned, or some other way. In any event it was still created by a bank following strict guidelines)

Back to one who wants to buy the house.

The builder will accept money in exchange for the house because he can turn that money in for his own personal goods and services. The buyer doesn't have all the money to buy it out right, so he's willing to go into debt for it, because he wants it. However, the builder will not accept timely payments for his labor. He wants the money all up front, so he can move on to his next project, and hopefully will not have to go into debt while creating his house masterpieces. He is one who refuses to move on to the next thing, unless he's been paid for all input sources that went into his creation.

What's the buyer to do? He goes to a source that has access to money. Enough so that he can buy the house. He goes to a bank, where an abundance of money is. In fact many people go to the bank for loans all at once on any given day.

One day fifty people went to the same bank around the same time for 150,000 dollar loans or more to purchase houses. That was a total of roughly 7.5 MM dollars. The owner of the bank realized he didn't have 7.5mm on hand, but sure did want to make those loans, so the money he lent out could go to work and earn interest, thereby earning him more money, of which he would give a tiny portion to the depositors for letting him use their money while holding it.

Enter the Federal Reserve, National Money Policy etc etc. The Federal Reserve, of which this banker is a member bank because he pays fees and invests in it for it's magical services, gives the banker permission to just create the shortfall out of thin air, provided he had say, one tenth of the actual money in dollars, on deposit or in some other liquid form in the bank's possession. Based on this rule, the banker checks his vault and finds he has 1MM dollars on hand, more than enough to cover the federal reserve guideline, so he invokes the magical powers being a member of the Federal Reserve allows him, and opens his accounting books to record the 50—150,000 dollar credit checks he writes to the customers that want to buy homes and becomes in a sense, **co-owner** with the customer, until the customer pays the 150,000 loan plus interest over time. Usually 30 years.

The buyer goes back to the builder and offers him the check the bank gave to him for payment and the builder accepts the check and hands over the house, because he trusts that in this day and age, the bank is good for it.

Let's look at this again. Based on the buyers' current ability to make projected/future repayments, the banker gets magic powers from the credit kings above him, to create this account. In fact, the banker has started an account for the buyer, backing the buyer up with the bank's good name, by co signing the debt, then offers the buyer up to the credit kings for sacrifice. Hopefully he has been programmed well enough over the years to be an obedient slave to payments. The buyer started in the ditch, by going into debt for the purchase of a house. But that's what he was taught to do.

After falling on some hard times, seven years later, the buyer is no longer able to afford payments on the house. The bank doesn't care. The bank doesn't really remember its victims over time. His house is foreclosed on by the bank, which means the bank takes sole ownership of it now and there are no longer any other parties involved to make claim against it. (The builder was paid up front, and the buyer, just couldn't cut it anymore). And even though in real dollars, when combining principal and interest payments together, the house is half way paid for, the bank doesn't care. It takes that one house, seemingly for free and becomes the selling agent, looking for another prospective borrower to start the process with all over again.

The banker realizes, if well maintained, this one house could be sold and resold many times like this, or better yet, someone could just pay the bank outright, the entire price of the home because they have alternative financing arrangements, and the bank will have made a handsome profit of all of buyer one's principal and interest, and the entire payment again (at an appreciated value), from the new buyer. Win Win for the bank.

But what about buyer one? 1). During the original transaction, the builder got his money up font, from a sort of bogus check, backed by the bank's credit reputation. The builder is happy. The transaction worked out well for him. 2). The buyer and the bank were co borrowers together on the transaction, of which only the buyer made payments into it. Sure he got to write off the interest and tax payments over those seven years, while in theory, the bank got to pay taxes on the principal and interest earnings the buyer paid into the deal, but why doesn't he own the house also? Why doesn't he also reap in the profits that the bank seems to wallow in? Why is he ruined with the credit king, unable to get anything on credit now? The credit he has become accustomed to. Why have we been taught to live through debt? Why has everything been taken away, priced and re-sold to the public? No one knows how to do anything anymore.

Anyway, my point is that banks work mainly on credit. The credit is their name and the form of institution they are. It is the most powerful institution on earth, back by some of the most powerful creative minds and organizations. The government supports it. The federal reserve supports it, and if failure seems imminent, we, the tax payer will support it, by government mandate, through taxes. It is also a corporation. The most powerful kind. It has the power to destroy the credit of individual humans if they don't play by the rules, and it also has the power to crush its corporate cousins, who are the brothers of human humans.

Yes, a bank says who of the human race, both real and created, have credit. Good or bad, and they have the wherewithal to label you and track you to the ends of the earth, making sure that other corporations and humans will be wary of doing business with you.

And forget the roots. My parents, starting behind the eight ball of according to the master plan, by having children first, bought their first house in 1973 and kept it for eighteen years, until most of us were gone. Then they moved to their second home where they have resided for the last 15 or so years.

The fad for our generation has been to look at your home purchase as an investment. With an investment, one wants returns. How do you get returns? By selling your house(What do you care about the community or neighborhood, or raising a family in a stable environment?)

Or if you want to stay in your home, another way to get some of that equity out is to refinance? (refer to the man on the lawnmower in the commercial).

But when we choose the first option as a return, what are we teaching the next generation, our kids? (In the current climate soon, we may even have to move out of the country to get jobs). We're teaching them that it's okay not to have roots or get used to life long friends, or get used to anything….. By the way, I'm only 36. I find it amazing that when I reflect, these are the things I see. That I can see change and realize I am apart of that uprooted generation being tossed to and fro by non stop change and I can tell you progress and change are different. Change is not always progress.

REPUBLICANS, DEMOCRATS, LEFTS, RIGHTS, REDS AND BLUES, CONSERVATIVES & LIBERALS

How lazy is that? How presumptuous of politicians to throw out labels and expect us to put one or more on. And to keep it on, and to vote blindly by color or word? To adopt theirs and the media's definition of what these, not even acronyms mean, and mold ourselves to it, for their ease and pleasure. I'm tired of this. Aren't you? Aren't you tired of hearing these words. Why can't the best man win? Why can't we discover what needs to be discovered and align ourselves to the best possible candidate for the job of leading this country. Why do they think we can't take these labels off? Why do they think we should be branded for life and generations by them? Why is that? What kind of thinking is that on their part? Moronic if you ask me. Are we all morons? I mean politicians claim whole states this way. Really, what the hell is that? Why can't a person like some of both ideologies, or more of one than the other, or even change his mind midstream through a campaign in light of new evidence?

I mean these are just pairs of words, representing the opposite ends of a continuum (like that word huh!), and each pair is synonymous with the other , even though when looking each word up separately in the dictionary you get a different meaning.

About this current administration, including everybody, republican or democrat, red or blue, left or right, I would advise us to just clean house and get some real and new thinking going on in there. They're a bunch of lazy, reactive, leeches. Looking only for comfort and security within the game. At this rate, Americans can be assured of losing their freedom. Or is it stature I'm thinking?

DEVIL'S ADVOCATE

After having said all that, I'd like to clarify that all corporations aren't bad. It's when they are allowed to grow unchecked, unpatriotic, and un American, and into this worldly thing. What's wrong with patriotism? What's wrong with staying true to your roots? Answer: Not enough money, if there is an opportunity to make more. It's also, not enough power within the power structure, if there is an opportunity somewhere else within someone else's power structure. Why do corporations have to have it all? I remember when I was in school, my history teacher said monopolies were bad. Bad for competition and fair pricing, so they were all but abolished, and now thanks to Mr. Reagan, they're back. If a corporation/industry is not immediately identifiable as a monopoly, it certainly is a cartel.

When I was in College late eighties or so, I had an International Finance professor who said things like, pretty soon there will be a debit card where people will use their own money accounts just like a credit card. He also said Europe would have a single currency. I just couldn't believe that nonsense. I thought his words were ambitious thoughts that would never come to pass. I was used to our current world at the time. I believed money in itself was special and that surely people wouldn't allow their actual money to be replaced by a card. I mean, we were talking about **money**. "PROFFESSOR CAN WE STICK WITH TODAY! THIS CLASS IS TOUGH ENOUGH."

"And I'll be damned," is all I can say now. Today is here. I think about him and wonder why he had the inside track, and if he were still lecturing, was he telling more about the future, and if so, where was he so I could hear and believe this time and get ready for it.

The point is, these changes that actually happened are bringing the economies of nations, consumers, sellers and all monetary actions in line to meet each other somewhere. Or better, they have done this already.

One big connection of ease. Woe to the criminal one day, when they no longer allow for paper money, but I'm sure he'll get creative as well.

Another point is that I should have been paying attention. As most teen and young twentiers, we are preoccupied with other stuff and we don't pay attention. So when you're in a class young people or anywhere, maybe reading the newspaper even, pay attention, the future might be being laid out right before your eyes. And you can determine then if it's to your liking, or at the very least determine how changes are going to affect your life and prepare for them or prepare to do something about change. I don't know. Just pay attention.

Personally, I find the debit card quite addictive, even useful. Sometimes I mistake it for a credit card. But I try to make an effort at remembering we used to not have them. And the euro, I've never seen one in person, but I hear it's causing confusion in its purpose to unite all the currencies of Europe. I'm not so sure how it will succeed in the end. There's some ego involved.

THE GREATEST ADDICTION IN ALL TIMES

What is this fake money interest
Created to help your fellow man
What is this fake money interest
That never touches hand

There's got to be more interest now than money
Is there any money left?

We're so creative even our money is a slave
Money go work off that interest you can't be saved!

And what are you saving it for anyway?
You can't take it to the grave.

FREE MONEY!!!!
Now there's a concept and a chant

FREE MONEY!!!!
It's lent/bought its way so far into the future
That you can't.

I'm sure it needs no introduction, but I'll give it one anyway. Just about everyone you meet is addicted to it in one form or another. The chaos, destruction and devisiveness it causes. It comes before family in many cases, because one will chase after it, and scheme for it almost to total destruction of whatever else he may have in his life. He grows up idolizing it because there never seems to be enough according to our parents and relatives. He's taught in school about its importance and how it makes the world go around. He covets it. He competes for it. It is the most powerful stuff on earth. Yet unlike a more tangible item, that is priced by supply and demand, there is almost no overhead to make it. It's practically made for free. But we trip over ourselves and each other trying to acquire it. Nothing is more important. Everything else can wait. This most powerful weapon on earth is sometimes perceived as greater than air, water, or health. This stuff is money. The American dollar. And we're going to have to learn to understand it better, so we can break the addiction. We need to understand what it does, how it grows, why it grows, and who keeps allowing it to grow. There's so much of it around these days, it's driving up the price of everything. There's too much of it out there. People are overdosing on it. With all that's out there, and more being sent out every day it defies the concept of simple supply and demand. But to the simple American, the reason this is so, is because of the rule of consumption. Our rule in America is to consume. The only way to consume seems to be by acquiring this stuff. The consumer mentality requires lots of money to work at optimal capacity. It's a mentality that often brings less than desirable results. Some symptoms of failure on this path are financial ruin, or financial creativity, financial fraud, burn out from overwork, and committing outright crimes against humanity to acquire more money or more stuff.

We however, can change our thinking about consumption. It's going to be hard though, with all of these enticing commercials touting empty benefits. If we stopped to think about ourselves and what one really needs to live off of, it doesn't veer from prior centuries. Food, clothing and shelter. Everything else is somebody's creative idea. Nothing else is that important. Nothing. If we stopped distracting ourselves with the belief that things are that important to have, we'd have more time. And in that time, we'd all be able to think more clearly. Lose the herd mentality, and not be so consumerish. I know our leaders say it is the American's job in the dynamic of the world economy to spend spend spend. But that doesn't make it true, or right. This ideology can be changed, and when it is, we can break our addictive habits and break the spell of money. We'd have more time for our loved ones, more time to be creative with our minds, instead of giving our bodies to some excessive work ethic, and we could all become nicer. We'd have more time to learn how to do things, that our forefathers once did for themselves, rather than buying it to be done. It seems every idea, thought, mechanism, resource, need, has been tied up by an organization or corporation and re sold to us. Things that often, if we had the time, we could or would do ourselves.

Not to mention, at the present time, we are in a recession, make no mistake about it. The consequences of all that consumer lending and consumer buying over the past few years is knocking at our door. 1929, ain't got nothing on what 's been going on, and if the Fed and financial industry decides to stop these ridiculous practices any time soon, coupled with jobs being lost, and lost to other countries, a lot of us will be in big trouble.

Where were the economists and financial strategists or just someone who could think and connect dots: I hear of all of these world economic forums, and you mean not one person present was aware of the debacle we were headed into here in America? **Fewer jobs, stagnant salaries and lower pay for new employees did not equal higher housing prices and easier than ever to get, no money down mortgages, with payments that increase over time**. Who allowed this? What was the purpose? The door to America was wide open and every country with a financial pulse bought into this strategy and lent money to the Americans.

I'll read the future like my college professor and tell you all that pretty soon the rubber band of the 'elastic' money system is going to pop. Where will you be?

Stopped to Think

One day in the late nineties, after feeling, beat down, and somewhat tired and abused, I quit my job(to find another of course), but in the process of deciding what new suit to wear, I woke up and realized I didn't want to be a bird singing in a cage. For the majority of my twenties, I lived in darkness; a slave to every day life and living, running myself ragged trying to perfect for myself, an obsolete formula of success. In this darkness the world I knew was changing and I couldn't even see it. From what I know now, the changes weren't even gradual in the sense of time. I just wasn't paying attention. I was too busy. But when I woke up, I discovered the very foundation of my formative years, the ethics, the morals and the taboos, had transformed in a 180 degree fashion. White men, those old dinosaurs who dominate the earth kind, were being challenged on every front and being forced into effecting the role of apologetic, reflective wimp. Women were choking on the results of their movement towards equality. They had effectively and single handedly killed chivalry and romance. Now women and men are fairly equal. Homosexuals were prominent and proud of it. They had successfully formed a powerful bloc and political coalition for themselves, often equating their circumstances with that of a fight similar to blacks and their cause for civil rights. They took civil rights and spread that to sexual orientation!

But racism still means to do what it always has, and is even bigger now, encompassing all of the different people of the entire global community and breaking them down into new ethnic categories. And, in America a new term called socio economics has also expanded from this. And people are still starving in Africa, as well as in other parts of the world, including America.

I pondered all of this and asked myself, where had my world gone. We now had smart computers and stupid people. No one it seems, knew how to think. Thinking had become a lost art. Unfortunate that was for me too, because like the bumper sticker read, I stopped to think, and then I never wanted to start again. I didn't want to start the game all over again. I didn't want to learn or embrace the new set of codes and ethics. There was no way my psyche would allow me to. I had to spread my wings and fly wherever they took me. No man or rules could change who I had already become. I escaped from the cage. I would never be put back in one. Now I am flying solo wondering where to go.

END WORDS

Being a child of parents reared in the south, (who transplanted themselves in urban enclaves in the north. Ghettos.) And growing up around other children of like situations,...and so add country colloquialism and dialect, ghetto slang with TV, and what is being said, and from its being said by authority figures in schools and other public arenas, and you get me. Someone, whom, when out of home element of country colloquialism and dialect, and the slang verbiage of peers, has to hold her hands to her head, close her eyes, and remember the words, context and pronunciation of the larger, more acceptable public. I've been doing this for over twenty-five years. You would think that I'd have adopted that way by now.

Their words are not my words. I don't talk like that, and if truth be told, they have too many words. I can feel myself transforming the night or moment before office meetings, or the seconds before responding to a client, superior or authority figure. The words roll around in my head. I search through the jargon databases and I come up with a response that sounds like what they all want to hear.

Every time it's like I'm getting into character. I remember in college on rubric type responses, whether good or bad in total (I laugh as I write the word rubric, for surely there is a more familiar way to say survey, or feedback).... anyway, my peers would often write "very well spoken," as though that's a real plus for me. I didn't want to be speaking like that, but I felt the situation called for that kind of speak.

And so what I am saying is that I transform. My voice changes. My demeanor and mannerisms change, and at the end of the day all I can think is how my favorite word is 'fuck.' Not in the sense of it being a curse word, but just, "fuck," (meaning something's not going the way I expected it to or "fuck it,"(meaning forget this man), or"fuck that,"(which means forget that), or "What the fuck," (which means, what is this, what are you doing, what the hell is going on, etc), or "who fucking cares?" (Which means what I said, but with extra emphasis and feeling to accentuate the depth to which I mean it), or "fuck off,"(which means leave me alone, or leave, or I don't believe you, etc.) or "Who gives a fuck," (which means who cares, I don't). Anyway, you know what I mean. That one word alone, or dressed up with a pronoun, noun , adjective, verb or adverb, or functioning in anyone of those capacities, conveys so many things, easily discernable to the recipient. Its meaning is never confused.

So why do we have so many words? I am convinced that each new word was created to cloud and convolute, to spin and to confuse the meaning of a previous word. To add to and to take away meaning. Why is a contract so convoluted? Why are there people who make a fine living out of being artsy with the interpretation of words? (I'm thinking lawyers). To be honest, we don't even use words correctly when speaking out loud. We're always only lying due to the subtraction and addition of meaning. We're only truthful in our minds. Whenever we speak outside of our minds, due to this addition and subtraction, most of the time we just lie. Because inside we can feel, and who can ever say out loud what they truly feel?

I guess I bring this up for a reason. Surely we think along certain lines for a reason. The reason I believe I am thinking this way is because I feel fucked (fooled over). Every one of those fuck phrases describes how I feel now, all the time on any given day. I'm also feeling like I just don't give a fuck (I don't care).

www.ingramcontent.com/pod-product-compliance
Lightning Source LLC
Chambersburg PA
CBHW050351290526
45785CB00006B/2720